Anni & Carsten Sennov

Spirit Mates
The New Time Relationship

I0540551

good adventures publishing

Spirit Mates - The New Time Relationship

©2014, Anni & Carsten Sennov and Good Adventures Publishing
First edition, first impression
Set with Cambria
Layout: Anni Sennov – www.good-adventures.dk
Cover Design: Michael Bernth – www.monovoce.dk
Author photo: Lisbeth Hjort – www.lisbethhjort.dk

Original title in Danish:
"Åndsdualitet - Den Nye Tids parforhold"
Translated into English by: David Tugwell
Proofread by: Sue Jonas Dupuis

ISBN 978-87-92549-56-3

Contents

Foreword

Have you ever wondered why you believe that you have met 'the one' only to have things fizzle out for no apparent reason? Why is it that some people just cannot make things work in a relationship despite their very best intentions? Do opposites really attract?

People the world over are searching for the perfect partner or are looking to improve their relationship with the existing one, maybe feeling a deep yearning inside which seems impossible to fulfill. Why does it seem so difficult for so many of them?

In this little book, Anni and Carsten Sennov provide some consciousness-based answers to these and other questions. As the couple behind AuraTransformation™, a once in a lifetime energy treatment which brings about a permanent expansion of your consciousness, they use their expertise to analyse the multiple aspects of love relationships and their link to the Universal Plan. First, they explain how relationships function from a traditional soul energy point of view. They then describe how the paradigm shift into spirit energy, currently taking place on planet Earth, heralds a new era of possibilities in love relationships and how you can benefit from this.

Whether you are still searching for the perfect match, or you are trying to understand the energy in your relationship, the information contained in this book will enlighten you and provide invaluable insights into how to go about getting what you want. If you have already found your spirit mate, you will have a more profound understanding of how everything comes together.

Happy reading! I wish you all the love in the world,

Sue Jonas Dupuis

The ideas behind the book

Love is a phenomenon that has always interested humanity. Much has been said, written and sung about love, and all kinds of positive and negative emotions have been expressed on the subject. Yet most people find it difficult to define exactly what it is that love means for them.

Since we, Anni and Carsten, have been fortunate in being able to meet as love partners and experience the unique consciousness-based love constellation which being spirit mates is all about, we have decided to share our experiences with others. Exactly what does love look like when it is experienced between two adults who, at the very beginning of time, were made for each other in an identical spiritual image?

Many things appear to be different in a relationship when it is based on spirit duality compared to what most of us are accustomed to from previous relationships. Therefore, this spirit duality should absolutely be experienced in real life, because it simply surpasses all your wildest dreams in every way.

If your one and only has yet to appear in your life, you could benefit from using the approach mentioned at the end of the book, which can help you to attract your spirit mate. It is quite certain that there is one spirit mate partner for all of us some-where out there who is more 'right' than any other love partner on our life path.
If, however, you are one of the lucky ones who has already met your spirit mate, this book is guaranteed to confirm everything about your relationship.

As a step on the path in its quest to bring everything in life back to its source, the Universe needs to bring together all spirit mates who originally grew out of the same cell division.

When the spirit and therefore love, is fully integrated into your consciousness, you cannot help but love yourself, and consequently also love your spirit mate. It is at this time when you will have the basis for being able to meet him/her here on Earth, which is the most life-affirming experience of all, beyond even that of bringing a child into the world.

We wish you all the best of luck in your relationship with that special someone, and in your search to find him or her if you have not yet succeeded in meeting each other physically here on Planet Earth...!

Anni & Carsten Sennov

Dear Reader,

If you like this book and want more information, I recommend you that you look at the website **www.annisennov.com** where you will find more information about new and forthcoming books in English, as well as upcoming lectures, workshops and courses throughout Europe. It is also possible for you to become a member of my English blog and to subscribe to my English newsletter, which is published several times a year. If you wish, you can also give personal feedback on books, lectures and personal consultations.

Loving Regards,
Anni Sennov

Soul mates

A person's spirit mate cannot in any way be compared to their soul mate or twin soul, which are now relatively well-known phenomena in spiritual circles, simply because two very different spheres of consciousness are involved.

The sphere of the soul is in fact contained within the sphere of the spirit and it has a connection to the Earth's previous reincarnation and karma system, where various personal relationships between people are agreed upon from one life to the next.

A relationship between two soul mates represents, as can be seen in the chart on page 13, an energy constellation between two often fundamentally different spiritual beings who, for reasons of consciousness development on Earth and in the name of wholeness, have agreed to stick together as love partners through several physical incarnations.

The soul partnership allows the two parties to feel bound to each other by fate, so that they can mingle their energies in their respective earthly lives over and over again, despite maybe having great basic personal differences.

In the context of the overall consciousness evolution on Earth, quite a lot of time is saved by allowing people to have the conviction that they are connected with one other person on the level of soul and destiny, and in some cases with multiple people spread over a whole lifetime. That way, it does not feel nearly as difficult for either of them to acquire personal skills and qualities that come from the other person's consciousness universe, even though these qualities may differ dramatically from their own original energy structure.

Soul energy is on the decline here on Earth, as all children from 1995 onwards have been born with only pure spirit energy in their aura - the Indigo and Crystal energies. That is why, from around 2010, we have begun to see more newly - established relationships based on spirit duality.

At this period in time, soul energy is solely related to the older generation.

Consciousness mates

Way back in time, it was possible to save a lot of time in the name of development by allowing people to have soul energy in their aura as well as a conviction that they were bound by fate with certain people. This set-up probably had its advantages, especially in the domain of personal development, where many people have been able to take bigger steps forward in life than they might otherwise have done, because they had a subconscious feeling that there was actually only one correct path to follow in life.

With the appearance of spirit energy here on Earth in every child's aura, as well as in each adult aura transformed through an AuraTransformation™ (see **www.auratransformation.com**), there is now the real possibility that all consciousness mates and then all spirit mates can actually meet each other in real life. Spirit mates will meet in order to start a love-based relationship on the earthly level.

It is certainly possible to meet a number of consciousness mates on your personal path of development. These consciousness mates may be of either sex, where the relationship presents itself as either a deep friendship or most often as a brief and very intense love affair that ends in nothing.

A consciousness mate relationship differs from a spirit mate relationship in that it is not totally sexually and physically focused. The sexual 'plug-and-socket' effect that makes the spirit mates' two bodies meld their respective spirit consciousnesses together into one shared spirit energy, is not found in consciousness mates, since their original spirit consciousnesses are not completely identical. We must stress, however, that a spirit mate relationship is not just purely sexual !

See the overviews on pages 13 and 23.

The energy similarity between consciousness mates occurs when each is following and exploring their individual personal development paths on Planet Earth but this does not mean that they are identical in spirit.

In the earthly sphere, even very small differences can separate consciousness mates from each other, sometimes in unpleasant and negative ways which may be totally disproportionate to the size of those differences. This can often be followed by great personal pain for both parties because they really want to open up to each other, but apparently cannot, despite their strong desire to do so.

The consciousness duality problem can be likened to attempting to open a door with a key that is cut slightly wrongly. The lock simply does not budge no matter how much you jiggle the key, as it is simply not the right key that you are trying to use.

On the spirit (non-earthly) plane, there are just not the same possibilities as there are here on Earth for mixing up the energies or even for dressing in a slightly different costume from your own. So on the spirit plane, this kind of scenario could only occur over a very short period of time.

It would just not be possible, therefore, to even imagine a scenario in which the end result would be getting together with the 'wrong' spirit mate

Consciousness mates only help each other to be whole by trying, on a consciousness level, to transfer their personal strengths and skills to each other through interaction, conversation, discussion and maybe transmission of thoughts.

Spirit mates

A person's spirit mate, or 'twin flame', is the other part of a person's spiritual energy from which he or she originated, on a consciousness level, back in the beginning of time, at the moment of the great cosmic cell division

Spirit duality can thus be traced back considerably further in the history of consciousness development than soul energy or consciousness duality. It corresponds to the spiritual interconnectedness between two cells and/or two people coming from that cell division.

In the great cosmic cell division, every cell always divided into two cells at a time, usually in the form of a masculine and a feminine energy which together represent a spiritual duality. It is this cell division which is now being restored to its spiritual source by the couple being brought together as love partners in their earthly lives.

The three different types of relationship - soul mate, consciousness mate and spirit mate – each represent different kinds of development between the two parties in the relationship (refer to the charts on pages 13 and 23). However, it can easily happen that a person has one and the same soul mate and spirit mate, or one and the same soul mate and consciousness mate. However, people never have the same consciousness mate and spirit mate. The consciousness duality represents only one step on the road to spirit duality.

The level of consciousness at which consciousness mates find themselves when they meet is always the same, hence the name and the reason for their meeting. However, the composition of their respective consciousnesses is not the same.

Spirit mates, however, have exactly the same consciousness structure and platform by virtue of their common origin in the spirit.

Spirit mates may well have met each other already at the soul level, but due to a partial or missing contact with the spiritual dimension they were not yet whole and in full balance. Therefore the couple were not able to jointly exploit the full potential of the relationship, which, further along the way, will lead to their common mission in life revealing itself.

Spirit mates have a deep, inner love for each another and often an inexplicable sense of cohesion that is not granted to soul mates, as the soul mate relationship is subject to external conditions in relation to certain earthly life paths and specific life tasks. However, this does not mean that soul mates cannot love each other deeply.

Consciousness and spirit mates can be difficult to distinguish from each other because they are energetically much more in synchrony with each other than are soul mates and spirit mates. The quickest way to spot the relationship is by observing how quickly imbalances arise in the relationship. In a spirit mate relationship it is in fact extremely difficult to disagree about anything at all, whereas there are often both small and large disagreements between consciousness mates due to them seeing things differently.

Out in the cosmos there is no such thing as soul energy and soul partnership, they are purely earthly phenomena whereas spirituality and spirit duality are not.

Soul energy and consciousness duality represent only a small step on the earthly path of development in the individual quest to become one with your total consciousness and its pure spiritual energy, and to finally be united with your ultimate spirit mate in both body and spirit.

Relationship types and characteristics

	Soul mates	Consciousness mates	Spirit mates
Facts	People with soul aura born before 1995	People with soul or new Indigo or Crystal aura	People with new Indigo or Crystal aura
Balance	On the way towards balance. Working with themselves to a greater or less degree	Shift between balance and imbalance due to small adjustments in their personality	Are in balance and whole
Partner	Are opposites	Are complementary	Are one in charisma, thoughts, action, and human values
Relationship	Complement, debate or fight with each other	Function as a step before the meeting with their spiritmate	Easiness in the relation Compatibility on all levels

The first meeting

When you meet your spirit mate for the first time, you can easily see that he/she is cute and looks really lovely but because your spirit mate has energy and charisma almost like your own, you may not necessarily perceive them as a potential love or marriage partner right away. Maybe you cannot even remember the person's name afterwards, only that they were so good to talk to or dance with or it was really pleasant to be in their company, and that they had a rhythm and a personal approach to life just like your own.

All that you can remember with certainty is that you got on fantastically well together in a purely human and perhaps a bodily way, and that there was extremely good chemistry between you. This chemistry was, however, only really noticeable to you when you made physical contact with each other via a handshake, a dance or touch in some other way. The spirit mate's physical presence - and not necessarily their appearance - made a much larger magnetic impression on you than the person's charisma did, since you already know your own so well !

When the first meeting between spirit mates takes place, the couple may not boast of having recognized each other instantly. However, everyone else can see a connection between the two spirit-connected people right away, without being able to understand why.

Everybody present, except for the spirit mate couple themselves, would have a clear and at the same time inexplicable feeling that 'something' is about to happen right in front of their eyes. This is because a spiritual fusion is about to take place on the consciousness level between the two spirit mates without anything being clearly visible on the outside. Then, the people around them often get a great unconscious urge to separate the couple.

This is especially true if one or both of the spirit mates' current relationship partners or close relatives are present at the first 'accidental' meeting.

Many unconscious scenarios can therefore begin to unfold at the spirit mates' first meeting without they themselves having the faintest idea that anything is going on. However, it is certain and has been shown, that they can always remember each other afterwards, even though they may have forgotten both the name and the exact appearance of the other person. Therefore it will not take long before the parties are completely inside the lives of each other as their respective spirit consciousnesses continue to merge, without the parties necessarily being totally aware of this on an everyday conscious level.

The consciousness fusion between spirit mates is simply unavoidable, and the result is that they merge into one common spirit energy whilst their physical bodies remain intact, so that after a short time together they are like two bodies and one spirit...

Pure love

For you, your spirit mate is the most beautiful person you have ever known.

For you, your spirit mate will always appear beautiful both on the inside and on the outside, although other people may have different views, and when you are with your spirit mate, you feel completely whole, strong and rested in your own energy and in your common energy.

Spirit mates have an unconditional acceptance of each other through their common spiritual source and their identical consciousness. Intuition, love, trust and confidence are thus key words in their daily dealings with each other, and there is never doubt about the partner's deepest intentions in any given situation. You might just as well doubt your own intentions, since both parties get their spiritual impulses from the same place.

It may surprise many people to learn that only a few spirit mates have got together as love partners around the globe, but the reason for this is pretty obvious.
It is hard work for many people to find a way into themselves and if they have not yet achieved balance and settled down with their own personality, it can be difficult, on a day to day basis, living with a copy of yourself who is constantly highlighting aspects of yourself that you have not yet been completely reconciled with.
Seeing your own personal characteristics played out in real life through another person can feel extremely confrontational, since we can only experience ourselves from the inside out, and not the other way round.

The precondition for the spirit mates being allowed to meet each other at all in the earthly sphere is that they both feel whole inside and are in full balance within themselves.

Only by being fully in balance with themselves can they be ready at the consciousness level to be united with their spirit mate who must also be whole inside and fully balanced. If not, both parties will be held back in their respective spheres of consciousness until it is the right time for them to unite.

In the period of life which precedes the great consciousness union between the two spirit mates, one party is most often in the earthly sphere, where they are living a so-called established life with good grounding and a relatively fixed framework for everyday life. The other party however, is located in some higher and more spiritual air layer with a lighter approach to life, where personal freedom is a high priority, so the concept of being established is considered as a downgrade.

So one party has his/her feet well planted in the ground while the other is flying around more or less in the sky.

For spirit mates who have already met at soul level, a huge clean-up is nearly always needed in the relationship when each becomes complete and comes into full harmony with themselves. They suddenly have to look at each other and their relationship with new eyes, within the context of pure spirit energy.

Often there may have been infidelity or other unpleasant experiences in the soul level relationship so the pair have been forced to break with their original vision of each other. Even if both parties are just as much spirit mates and have been from the very beginning, their relationship cannot expand from soul level into being a relationship based on spirit duality without getting help from the outside world.

The elements missing in the relationship between the two soul mates so that each can become whole and meet as spirit mates need to come from somewhere. This often takes place through either spiritual or physical infidelity, where one or both parties in the relationship enter into a close relationship with one or more consciousness mates on their path. It is therefore not without reason that the subsequent clean-up efforts can need to be enormous.

Some spirit mates may have been 'lucky' to be able to come together as soul mates early in life. But maybe they are not so lucky, as many illusions, memories and (mis)conceptions about each other from old times, need to be examined and transformed and then be erased forever to make room for the new spirit-based view of each other.
As spirit mates, the parties must be able to meet on a whole new basis of joint consciousness, founded on unconditional love, with no grudges or 'skeletons in the closet' from the past.

Interconnectedness
in the spirit

Spirit mates have an innate mutual sense of unity and an unconditional acceptance of each other and they basically agree on everything in their everyday lives.

Spirit mates each have their own approach to life due to their often very different life experiences, and this can be most obvious at the beginning of the relationship. It is therefore very rare that any kind of argument breaks out between the couple, and if an issue should come up for debate - and not for argument - then they will quickly reach agreement, as it most often will be just a matter of choice of words that separates them.

We could say that the spirit mates each come from their individual place in life, but not from their own individual place in consciousness. At spirit level, they are located in exactly the same place and have always been connected with each other in their inner core. However, this is not something that either of them have been aware of during their multiple earthly lives, which explains why many people walk around with a big unconscious feeling of longing deep inside. It is a longing that cannot be defined, but which many people feel very strongly if they have not yet succeeded in meeting their spirit mate in real life. To put it simply: every human being, either consciously or unconsciously, longs to meet their spirit mate - the person with whom they originated in the spirit and who is completely identical to them in the structure of their being.

Despite all the beautiful states and experiences that it is possible to have with one's spirit mate, there are very few adults with the necessary respect for themselves to allow themselves to choose to live with a carbon copy of themselves, who is just in another body, on a daily basis. Many people cannot see the benefit of being together with another person who behaves just like them, unless they want to live in a commune, where a common approach to things is seen as an advantage.

Instead, most people seem to get turned on by their opposites, by the qualities of another person that they do not already possess themselves. In relationships, people on Earth have always unconsciously sought to connect with their own consciousness counterpoint in the form of a soul mate, so that both could become more complete and able to overcome obstacles in daily life. However, now things are changing.

The history of human evolution has now come so far that it is time for individuals to consciously begin to unite with the other part of themselves.

Not with their other half, but with *their other part*, which is quite conveniently located in another body often of the opposite sex, although obviously not for homosexuals.

Now it is possible to create a consciousness and love-based attraction between two spirit mate bodies, which outwardly looks like a plug and a socket that fit perfectly together.

Thus when the two spirit mate bodies come into contact with each other, they can generate a great deal of extra energy for their joint benefit, as well as bringing the spirit mates' two identical consciousnesses together into one larger joint consciousness energy. In this way, the spirit mates may jointly feel even more whole as a couple than they have ever felt as individuals, because love is constantly flowing freely between them, and because their consciousness merging and connectedness ensures that they can never be separated from each other ever again.

They have thus reached home.

**Anything that is rightfully connected in spirit
can never be separated by any human on Earth.**

No matter how much you conjure, use magic or hocus-pocus, it is totally impossible to separate those particles and elements that belong together in spirit. Similarly, it is impossible to continue to keep particles and elements from joining if they have exactly the same spiritual source.

If the current separation between the various particles and people with the same spiritual source was constantly maintained, it would never be possible to lead the universes back to their origin out in the cosmos, and so we might as well immediately abandon all spiritual development and enlightenment here on Earth.

In the deep love relationship that spirit duality is, there are always streams open for sending and receiving love and intuitive impulses between the couple. The spirit mates' respective consciousnesses have, right from the start, been working diligently to melt into one common consciousness, and once this merger is complete, it is totally impossible for either of the parties to even periodically close off the exchange of energy and love between each other.

Once the spirit mates' respective consciousnesses are fused together, and they have entered into a deeper love with each other, they cannot always clearly feel the presence of the other's consciousness unless they are in the same room.
It may therefore be necessary, on a daily basis, to agree on one or more ways to get in consciousness contact with each other if the phone or computer is not close by. This is because if one spirit mate sends their thoughts towards the other, then the receiver may very well believe that it is their own thoughts they are registering, as the consciousness and thought pool

that is used is the same for both of them.

In fact, the spirit partner's heart is the only safe place to go with your impulses when you want to be in consciousness contact with your spirit mate, as the heart speaks the language of love and honesty, so there is no risk of you believing that it is your own thoughts when in fact it is your spirit mate who is thinking of you.

Relationship types and companionship

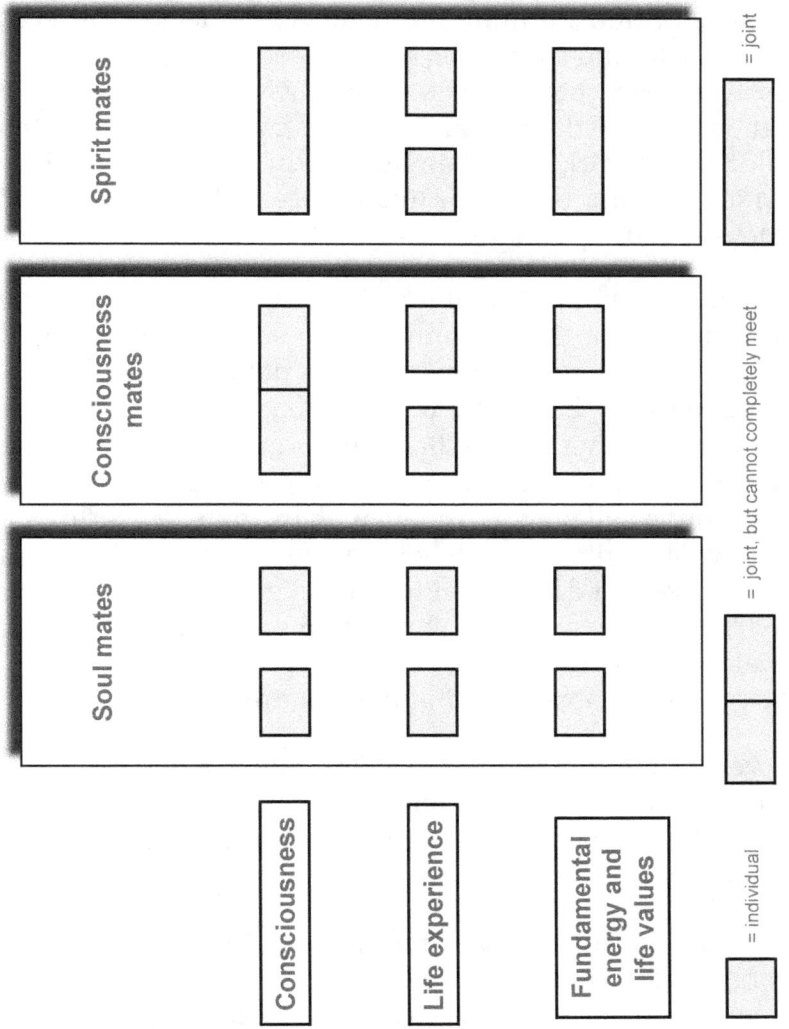

It could not have happened before

Because of God's infinite intelligence, He decided to wait to bring spirit mates together on the earthly level until He was absolutely sure that each of them had lived their respective lives to the fullest, with their various daily commitments related to children and work, etc., Then He wouldn't run the risk of having two spirit-connected people totally obsessed with each other on all levels, and especially on a sexual level.

If it had been possible to unite all spirit mates, on the physical level, right from the beginning when soul energy was still in operation, from a pure consciousness point of view the couple would not have been able to work constructively together in everyday life. There would have been a great danger that due to their inevitable consciousness merging, the spirit mates would have stopped all human contact with the outside world.
They would quite simply have been enough for each other and would have found it very difficult to let go of each other in daily life. That has never been a part of God's overall plan for human development here on Earth.
The goal is not obsession, but unconditional love.

However, in the old soul-based world, spirit duality could easily turn into physical and personal obsession if any couple were to meet, with its full consciousness potential, before being fully in balance themselves.

In the old world, until around the year 2000 - when the soul energy was in control and relationships were based on a consciousness attraction and balance between opposites – also called soul partnerships - spirit mates would have had a real reason to fear that they would lose a part of themselves if they surrendered completely to love and to each other. It is in some way true that they would have lost themselves under these circumstances, since soul energy can be very individualistic and often ego-oriented. This is why spirit mates would have risked becoming jealous, instead of providing space for true love in their relationship.

Unlike soul energy, spirit energy corresponds to a person's full consciousness potential. This energy allows space for a more flexible, comprehensive and holistic way of being, as well as a deep respect for each individual.
On the physical level, spirit energy concerns itself with the person's body and their vigour as well as all the possible ways they can have of being able to express energy.
On the spirit level, no consideration is given to the individual's old ways of thinking. Certain emotions, which could previously have made people act inappropriately in the company of others are not given consideration. With spirit energy, each and every individual is expected to have let go of all their old soul-based energies and ways of behaving, since at soul level people didn't mind letting any personal imbalances play out in relation to the whole.
Instead, it is expected that people will always seek an overall positive development for the benefit of the whole, whilst simultaneously preserving their own energy.

Both now and in the future, when spirit energy is the predominant energy on Planet Earth, people will be able to solve their own problems and feel inner peace, according to their personal internal and external situation at that moment.

**All actions should be consistent with
your current internal and external situation.**

If a person can master the art of action and state of being in this way, whilst also being in full personal balance, and if they can renounce their soul consciousness in favour of pure spirit, which happens via an AuraTransformation™, then this person has every chance of meeting their spirit mate on Earth.

In the spirit world, people with the same energy are always attracted to each other, so it is now possible for like to meet like in the name of love.

Spirit duality
in the relationship

With soul energy, everything is predetermined down to the very last detail, and all human thoughts and actions are completely attuned to the whole in order for the huge earthly and karmic jigsaw puzzle to move into a higher frequency based on fairness. Spirit energy and spirit mates however represent a free-flowing love energy which can seem highly unpredictable for many people.

Spirit energy thus offers a wealth of opportunities in life that the couple may explore in each other's company. A normal day in the name of spirit duality is rarely completely predictable. However, the couple has a common life purpose, of which they are not always aware at first. They must find this life purpose together by opening their hearts to each other.

For all spirit mate couples it is very important that they have a good balance between the inner and outer worlds in their relationship. Even a tiny variation in the relationship is noticed with lightning speed by both parties in their different ways, whether these small changes take place in the visible or the invisible world.
It takes the couple some time therefore, to adapt their thoughts and actions to meet the new conditions for living together, where the couple gradually tune in to each other's similarities and differences, the latter being influenced by the couple's previous imprinting in life due to upbringing, past relationships and the like.

Very often the couple's energies will circulate between them for several days without them being able to perform even the most basic activities, such as filling the dishwasher. At the beginning of the relationship, the couple need to make a great deal of effort when together to not be physically connected twenty four hours a day.

They can hardly bear to let go of each other, so it is imperative that the external world should at least occasionally call on one or both of them so that they can be separated.

In particular, many men with the old soul energy in their aura will probably envy the spirit mates their kind of partnership where bodily contact, touching and sex often have a very high priority and so make up a large part of their everyday interaction. The 'plug and socket' metaphor, which we used earlier, really does apply, in both heterosexual and homosexual relationships.

With this plug-and-socket effect, spirit mates can and do accumulate a large amount of consciousness and bodily energy by bringing their bodies together at least once a day, so they often have a hard time keeping their hands off each other for any length of time.

As their consciousnesses are already united and therefore forever linked, bodily contact can only support this spiritual connectedness in the most beautiful way.

It is unconditional love that is expressed when the couple have sex, and that is why the dream of being with your one and only suddenly takes on an even greater meaning.

It is possible for infidelity to occur as long as one of the partners in the relationship is still in the old soul sphere of consciousness and is not yet fully settled with him or herself, and the other party is in the spirit sphere corresponding to the new era of energy. However, infidelity is never an option when both parties have upgraded to the spirit energy and their consciousnesses are fused together.

If you look at the spirit mates' individual physical and personal characteristics, you can see that they are often very similar to each other. They are not necessarily completely identical in appearance, but due to the equality of their energy, you could be led to believe that they might be related to each other, which, in a way, they are. Except that they are spiritually related rather than physically related.

In the sexual relationship, this similarity is often evident, as the couple are perfectly compatible in a bodily way and they have the desire to do the very same things for and with each other. One of the spirit mates will bring energy from below thanks to their good earthly connection, while the other will bring energy from above with their greater connection to the spiritual dimension. This will continue until the couple have exchanged so much energy that they can each get energy both from above and below. This leads to the possibility of an orgasm, which is both internal and external, which cannot be described with mere words. It needs to be experienced.

The common mission in life

All spirit mate couples have a common mission in life, which they are expected to fulfil during their earthly relationship with each other. The fulfilment of this precise overall life purpose is the main reason that spirit mates get to meet each other and to live together on Planet Earth.

For God Himself knows what great consciousness strength a spirit mate couple can produce together in the world through their unconditional love for each other! The power that is being mobilized when each partner allies their energy resources with people with a different consciousness background is insignificant in comparison with the allied spirit energy force.

The actual results of this life goal are not predetermined, and neither is the path that the spirit mate couple are expected to move along together to realize their common life purpose.

All the initiatives that the spirit mate couple take jointly along the way to fulfilling their mission in life are honoured and supported from a spiritual side as much as possible, as long as the result best meets the consciousness and human development of the whole and all parties involved.

The person in the spirit mate relationship with the strongest earthly connection from the outset, may easily have sensed their common life mission deep inside many years before the couple were able to meet, where it has remained as a kind of future coding in the consciousness.

The other partner, who would most often have had a more conscious spiritual approach to life, will instead have seen their life task as a vision that they expected to live out sometime in the future.

In order for spirit mates to identify their common great mission in life, there are some relationship phases that they must first pass through:

1. The couple have to choose each other as love partners regardless of the extent of external resistance.
   However, this choice is not normally very difficult
   for spirit mates to make even though those around
   them can create a lot of unconscious resistance
   which shows itself in many ways.

2. Then, and fairly quickly, they will together create
   a framework for everyday life and a joint physical
   platform in the outer world, corresponding to the
   consciousness standpoint they have together on
   the spirit level. This provides peace and security
   in the relationship and daily life in order to be
   able to take care of things other than just tuning
   into each other's energies and immediate state of
   mind.

   There are very few people who can devote 100%
   of their time and thoughts to just one other person,
   which is why planning, prioritizing, and a sense of
   order are appropriate ingredients in a relationship if you do not want to risk everything in life
   floating away from you. Floating is something that
   can very rapidly happen in a spirit mate relation
   where the partners unconditionally follow each
   other, often without special consideration for the
   practical side of life.

3. As a key factor in the joint mission being revealed
   to them, the couple go through a stage in the rela-

tionship where they open their hearts completely to each other so that they can fully unite with their cores and their common life purpose, which is hidden deep within in both of their hearts.

Only with love and by opening both hearts simultaneously and collectively will their common life purpose present itself, so that the realization of their goal in life can begin in the outer world.

The path to your spirit mate

Even if you have not yet met your spirit mate here on Earth, you can do something yourself to accelerate this connection on the spirit level, and in this way create the basis for an earlier meeting with your one and only.

However, it is important to keep in mind that your spirit mate will not just pop up in your life simply because you send an order to God that he should send the person to you at once. Selfish actions are not rewarded - they are a sign that you are not yet pure in your consciousness, and therefore not ready to be joined with your spirit mate yet.
It is your inner intentions and consciousness standpoint that are assessed when it is almost time to be joined with your spirit mate, so that you can both embark on a new era of consciousness in life.

The first step on the path is to find balance within yourself. This is done through self-development and can be helped by various personal development and boundary-stretching courses, etc. Because of the size of this subject, however, we will not go into the very specific development paths that may be best for you as you are probably already well under way in your personal development. Otherwise, you would probably never have started reading this book !

You have to follow your own way through the personality-development jungle by constantly tuning into your heart and listening in order to find the right answer for you. You will have no joy from walking paths recommended by others if they do not feel right on the inside. However, we can definitely recommend that you get an AuraTransformation™ as part of your personal development. For with an AuraTransformation™ you will have the New Time spirit-based consciousness structure integrated into your aura, which makes it possible for you to meet on an equal level with your spirit mate. However, this **does not** mean that you will then automatically meet your spirit mate.

The AuraTransformation™ is a significant step on the path to meeting this person in real life here on Earth, and it will help in many ways to speed up your personal development process considerably.

The next step in your personal development path follows when you feel that you are in complete balance with yourself. Then you can send out the following thought:

"Where are you my spirit mate? I am ready to meet you!"

This thought consists of two elements – it is both a request as well as an ultimate message that you are ready to meet your one and only.

Sending out the thought can take place anytime and anywhere. God and the overall consciousness in the Universe will do the rest when the time is right. However, you can amplify the power of the message if you mobilize all your energy when you send out the thought. Give yourself plenty of time and send the thought out at reasonably constant intervals. This is a way to affirm both for yourself and for the Universe that you are aware and serious with regard to achieving your desire to meet your spirit mate.

Your spirit mate will unconsciously pick up the signal, as it will act as an inner voice that calls to him or her. The further your spirit mate has advanced in their personal development towards inner balance, the sooner you will meet each other. Your call will get your spirit mate to unconsciously speed up their own development process in order to get into balance more quickly and be ready to meet you. The deep-seated longing to meet their one and only that everyone has inside them will now come to the surface and get your spirit mate to further accelerate their consciousness development.

In this way the Universe will bring you together when you are both ready and in place in your own energies.

As we said earlier, there do not need to be any big sparks between you at your first meeting, as there probably needs to be some fine-tuning between you. This is work that goes on behind the scenes and is not always visible to the spirit mates themselves. However, the couple will quickly detect a mutual recognition and a feeling of equality, and from there things will speed up by themselves.

All you have to do is take action and follow the flow and then you will experience the ultimate love and a feeling of ease in the relationship.

Now you have found your spirit mate and you will never let go of each other again...

The authors

Anni Sennov

Anni Sennov is a clairvoyant advisor, international lecturer and the author of more than 20 books about energy and consciousness, the New Time children and relationships, several of which have been translated from Danish into a number of languages.

Visit **www.good-adventures.com**

Anni Sennov was born in Denmark in 1962 and originally began her career in the financial world. Since 1993 she has had her own practice of personal counselling. Her great strength is her ability to clairvoyantly perceive multiple relevant circumstances pertaining to her clients' personality and consciousness.

Anni Sennov's work and books are mentioned in numerous magazines, newspapers, and have featured on radio and television in many countries, both in and outside of Europe.

Read more at **www.annisennov.com**

Anni Sennov is the woman behind AuraTransformation™, which is a powerful method for expanding your consciousness. She is also the founder of the Aura Mediator Courses™ which take place in different countries, mainly in Europe.

Visit **www.auratransformation.com**

Together with her husband Carsten Sennov, she is a partner in the management consulting and coaching company SennovPartners, where she is a consultant in the fields of personal development, energy and consciousness.

Visit **www.sennovpartners.com**

Carsten Sennov

Carsten Sennov was born in Denmark in 1962 and is managing partner of SennovPartners. He works there as a coach and advisor for leaders in smaller and larger companies He is also responsible for the company's franchise-based spiritual training business internationally.

As CEO and co-owner of Good Adventures Publishing, Carsten Sennov is responsible for publishing and selling the company's books, which are available in many languages.

Carsten Sennov was most recently Deputy CEO at Capgemini Denmark, where he was employed from 1999 to 2003.

During the period 1991-1998 he worked for Gartner; the last four years being based in Sydney, Australia, where he was Operations Director at Gartner Measurement Asia Pacific, Gartner's Benchmarking and Best Practice Division.

Carsten Sennov he has been a sportsman at an elite level and has travelled extensively. His exploits include sailing across the Atlantic Ocean in a riverboat and later on, travelling six months in the Australian Outback. He has worked very extensively in personal development.

Visit **www.sennovpartners.com**

Together Anni and Carsten Sennov have developed the personality type indicator four element profile™ that consists of four main energies corresponding to the four elements of Fire, Water, Earth and Air, which are each present in everyone in different amounts and with different balances. A number of courses are available on how to integrate, understand, read and communicate using the four elements both for personal use as well as for businesses.

Read more at **www.fourelementprofile.eu**

Other titles

Current books written by Anni & Carsten Sennov:

Spirit Mates - The New Time Relationship *(English)*
Henkikumppanuus – uuden aikakauden suhde *(Finnish)*
Andedualitet - Den Nya Tidens förhållande *(Swedish)*

Get Your Power Back Now! *(English)*
Tag din kraft tilbage nu! *(Danish)*
Récupère ton pouvoir maintenant! *(French)*
Ta tilbake kraften din nå! *(Norwegian)*
Ta tillbaka din kraft nu! *(Swedish)*

The Little Energy Guide 1 *(English)*
Malý energetický průvodce 1 *(Czech)*
Den lille energiguide 1 *(Danish)*
Väike energia teejuht 1 *(Estonian)*
Pieni energiaopas 1 *(Finnish)*
Le petit guide de l'énergie 1 *(French)*
Den lille energiguiden 1 *(Norwegian)*
Мини-руководство по работе с энергией, часть 1 *(Russian)*
Den lilla energiguiden 1 *(Swedish)*

(Be a Conscious Leader in your own Life)
Bliv bevidst leder i dit eget liv *(Danish)*
Bli medveten Ledare i ditt eget liv *(Swedish)*

Current books written by Anni Sennov:

Balance on All Levels with the Crystal and Indigo Energy *(English)*
Balance på alle planer med krystal- & indigoenergien *(Danish)*
Kristalli- ja indigoenergiat ja kokonaisvaltainen tasapaino *(Finnish)*
Balanse på alle plan med krystall- og indigoenergien *(Norwegian)*
Balans på alla plan med kristall- och indigoenergin *(Swedish)*

The Crystal Human and the Crystallization Process Part I *(English)*
The Crystal Human and the Crystallization Process Part II *(English)*
Krystalmennesket & Krystalliseringsprocessen *(Danish)*
Kristallmänniskan och Kristalliseringsprocessen *(Swedish)*

Crystal Children, Indigo Children and Adults of the Future *(English)*
Kristall-lapsed, indigolapsed ja uue ajastu täiskasvanud *(Estonian)*
Кристальные дети,дети Индигои взрослые нового времени *(Russian)*
Kristallbarn, indigobarn och framtidens vuxna *(Swedish)*

Love, Sex and Attraction - A Short Guide to a Successful Relationship *(English)*
Hvor svært kan det være? *(Danish)*

(Karma-free in the New Time)
Karmasta vapaana uuteen aikakauteen *(Finnish)*
Karmafri i den nya tiden *(Swedish)*

Sold out titles can be found at www.annisennov.com.

Related books

Balance on All Levels with the Crystal and Indigo Energy
by Anni Sennov

Get Your Power Back Now!
by Anni & Carsten Sennov

See www.amazon.com and others

www.ingramcontent.com/pod-product-compliance
Lightning Source LLC
Chambersburg PA
CBHW061721120626
46550CB00003B/1320